Xi Jinping on the Global Stage
Chinese Foreign Policy
Under a Powerful but Exposed Leader

COUNCIL *on*
FOREIGN
RELATIONS

International Institutions and
Global Governance Program

Council Special Report No. 74
February 2016

Robert D. Blackwill and Kurt M. Campbell

Xi Jinping on the Global Stage
Chinese Foreign Policy
Under a Powerful but Exposed Leader

The Council on Foreign Relations (CFR) is an independent, nonpartisan membership organization, think tank, and publisher dedicated to being a resource for its members, government officials, business executives, journalists, educators and students, civic and religious leaders, and other interested citizens in order to help them better understand the world and the foreign policy choices facing the United States and other countries. Founded in 1921, CFR carries out its mission by maintaining a diverse membership, with special programs to promote interest and develop expertise in the next generation of foreign policy leaders; convening meetings at its headquarters in New York and in Washington, DC, and other cities where senior government officials, members of Congress, global leaders, and prominent thinkers come together with Council members to discuss and debate major international issues; supporting a Studies Program that fosters independent research, enabling CFR scholars to produce articles, reports, and books and hold roundtables that analyze foreign policy issues and make concrete policy recommendations; publishing *Foreign Affairs*, the preeminent journal on international affairs and U.S. foreign policy; sponsoring Independent Task Forces that produce reports with both findings and policy prescriptions on the most important foreign policy topics; and providing up-to-date information and analysis about world events and American foreign policy on its website, CFR.org.

The Council on Foreign Relations takes no institutional positions on policy issues and has no affiliation with the U.S. government. All views expressed in its publications and on its website are the sole responsibility of the author or authors.

Council Special Reports (CSRs) are concise policy briefs, produced to provide a rapid response to a developing crisis or contribute to the public's understanding of current policy dilemmas. CSRs are written by individual authors—who may be CFR fellows or acknowledged experts from outside the institution—in consultation with an advisory committee. The committee serves as a sounding board and provides feedback on a draft report. It usually meets twice—once before a draft is written and once again when there is a draft for review; however, advisory committee members, unlike Task Force members, are not asked to sign off on the report or to otherwise endorse it. Once published, CSRs are posted on www.cfr.org.

For further information about CFR or this Special Report, please write to the Council on Foreign Relations, 58 East 68th Street, New York, NY 10065, or call the Communications office at 212.434.9888. Visit our website, CFR.org.

To submit a letter in response to a Council Special Report for publication on our website, CFR.org, you may send an email to CSReditor@cfr.org. Alternatively, letters may be mailed to us at: Publications Department, Council on Foreign Relations, 58 East 68th Street, New York, NY 10065. Letters should include the writer's name, postal address, and daytime phone number. Letters may be edited for length and clarity, and may be published online. Please do not send attachments. All letters become the property of the Council on Foreign Relations and will not be returned. We regret that, owing to the volume of correspondence, we cannot respond to every letter.

This report is printed on paper that is FSC ® Chain-of-Custody Certified by a printer who is certified by BM TRADA North America Inc.

Contents

Foreword

This Council Special Report by Robert D. Blackwill and Kurt M. Campbell, two experienced practitioners and long-time observers of American foreign policy, is based on a straightforward premise: Xi Jinping is the most powerful Chinese leader since Deng Xiaoping, one who has taken a number of steps to limit collective leadership and the political clout of the army. But the authors also argue that this same concentration of power is a double-edged sword, one that leaves President Xi exposed and potentially vulnerable to internal political challenge.

The vulnerability comes from several sources, but none is more critical than a slowing economy. The trajectory of the Chinese economy is the subject of active debate among outside experts, but there is consensus that China is experiencing a substantial slowdown and will not be able to regain the high rates of growth that characterized the last several decades.

The report suggests the possibility of greater political repression at home if there are signs the economic slowdown is triggering political instability. But the authors go on to note that Xi may as well be tempted to turn to foreign policy to redirect domestic attention away from a lagging economy, in the process burnishing his nationalist credentials. They anticipate continued Chinese pressure on neighbors in the East and South China Seas and are skeptical China will use the leverage it has over North Korea or assume more than a limited role in global governance. They do, however, expect China to continue to engage in selective institution building. Overall, they foresee a Chinese foreign policy that is assertive, coordinated, and diversified, one that constitutes a significant challenge to U.S. interests.

In response, Blackwill and Campbell call for a new American grand strategy for Asia, one that seeks to avoid a U.S.-China confrontation but to maintain U.S. primacy. Believing we are entering a critical moment in the evolution of China's relationship with the region and the world, the authors put forward a ten-point plan designed to shape what China does and how it does it. The two explicitly say they are not advocating a strategy of containment, which they dismiss as "a U.S.-Soviet concept that has no relevant application to East Asia today." Instead, they want the United States to make use of a variety of the instruments of state-craft "to incentivize China to commit to a rules-based order but impose costs that are in excess of the gains Beijing would reap if it fails to do so."

I want to highlight one last point that figures in this Council Special Report, one being published during a presidential campaign. To the extent there is a foreign policy debate, much of it focuses on the Middle East and, to a lesser extent, Russia. The authors of this report push back against such an emphasis, calling on U.S. policymakers to "recognize every day that the primary engines of the world economy and the challenge to American primacy are not in the Middle East or Europe but have shifted to Asia." It is a perspective and a corrective well worth considering.

As even this brief foreword should make clear, there is much to reflect on as regards both China and the United States in this Council Special Report. It should be read and debated by specialists and generalists alike as it raises many of the most important questions and issues at the core of the American foreign policy debate and raises them in a direct, challenging way.

Richard N. Haass
President
Council on Foreign Relations
February 2016

Acknowledgments

We would like to express our gratitude to the many people who made this report possible. To begin, we thank CFR President Richard N. Haass and Director of Studies James M. Lindsay for their support of this project and insightful feedback throughout the drafting process. We are in debt to the members of the CFR study group on Chinese foreign policy for their comments and critiques on our draft report, all of which improved the substance of the final text. The report also benefited from interviews conducted with current and former U.S. government officials, as well as insights from researchers and journalists immersed in the U.S.-China relationship.

We are grateful for the valuable assistance of Patricia Dorff, Eli Dvorkin, and Elizabeth Dana in CFR's Publications Department for their editorial support, and to members of the Global Communications and Media Relations team for their marketing efforts. We also appreciate the contributions of the David Rockefeller Studies Program staff in shepherding the report. We are especially grateful to Rush Doshi of Harvard University for his research and writing assistance. We also thank CFR Research Associates Lauren Dickey, a gifted sinologist, and Matthew Lester, as well as Ryan Oliver of the Asia Group.

This publication is part of CFR's International Institutions and Global Governance program and has been made possible by the generous support of the Robina Foundation. The statements made and views expressed are solely our own.

Robert D. Blackwill
Kurt M. Campbell

Acronyms

ADIZ	Air Defense Identification Zone
AIIB	Asian Infrastructure Investment Bank
BMD	ballistic missile defense
BRICS	Brazil, Russia, India, China, South Africa
CCP	Chinese Communist Party
CEO	chief executive officer
CICA	Conference on Interaction and Confidence-Building Measures in Asia
DPP	Democratic Progressive Party
EEZ	exclusive economic zone
EU	European Union
FTA	free trade agreement
G20	Group of Twenty
GDP	gross domestic product
LAC	Line of Actual Control
NGO	nongovernmental organization
PLA	People's Liberation Army
PRC	People's Republic of China
RCEP	Regional Comprehensive Economic Partnership
SOE	state-owned enterprise
TPP	Trans-Pacific Partnership
UN	United Nations
WTO	World Trade Organization

Council Special Report

Introduction

"He has iron in his soul."
—*Lee Kuan Yew, former prime minister of Singapore,
on Chinese President Xi Jinping*

Xi Jinping is the most powerful Chinese leader since Deng Xiaoping, and with his sweeping actions and ambitious directives he has fundamentally altered the process by which China's domestic and foreign policy is formulated and implemented. Xi's popular anticorruption campaign has cowed senior party and military officials and allowed him to amass dominating power in a short span of time. With this transcending authority, Xi has ended China's carefully evolved collective and consensual leadership structure, marginalized the bureaucracy, and put himself at the center of decision-making on all consequential matters.

This report discusses Xi's transformation of China's domestic politics, his background and beliefs, the challenges he faces from China's slowing economy, and the implications of his foreign policy for the United States.

One downside to Xi's breathtaking success in consolidating power is that it has left him with near total responsibility for his government's policy missteps on matters ranging from the stock market slowdown to labor market unrest. His visibility on these issues and his dominance of the decision-making process have made him a powerful but potentially exposed leader. With Xi's image and political position vulnerable to China's economic downturn, his country's external behavior may increasingly be guided by his own domestic political imperatives.

For the last three years, with China's economy still producing robust growth numbers, such concerns have not fundamentally influenced Xi's foreign policy. Xi has been able to be continuously proactive, and he has used his power to take China's foreign policy in a new direction. He has boldly departed from Deng's injunction to keep a low profile and has reclaimed islands, created international institutions, pressured neighbors, and deployed military assets to disputed regions. Xi's foreign policy has been assertive, confident, and, importantly, a diversified mix of both hard and soft elements. Even as China has taken firm steps on territorial issues, it has used geoeconomic instruments to offer generous loans and investments, and even created new organizations such as the Asian Infrastructure Investment Bank (AIIB).[1] By combining inducements with intimidation, Xi has demonstrated the benefits of cooperating with China as well as the economic and military costs of opposing it, especially on issues important to Beijing.[2]

Today, China's thirty-year era of 10 percent annual growth appears to have ended, with official statistics placing gross domestic product (GDP) growth below 7 percent, the government reducing its growth target to 6.5 percent, and a number of major banks and respected forecasters arguing the true growth rate is far lower—and will remain below 5 percent for years.[3] In light of this deepening economic slowdown, the future trajectory of Xi's external policy is in question. Some elements, including China's geoeconomic policies, will endure; nevertheless, China's foreign policy may well be driven increasingly by the risk of domestic political instability. For this reason, Xi will most probably stimulate and intensify Chinese nationalism—long a pillar of the state's legitimacy—to compensate for the political harm of a slower economy, to distract the public, to halt rivals who might use nationalist criticisms against him, and to burnish his own image. Chinese nationalism has long been tied to foreign affairs, especially memories of foreign domination and territorial loss.

For example, Xi may be less able or willing to compromise in public, especially on territorial issues or other matters that are rooted in national sentiment, for fear that it would harm his political position. He may provoke disputes with neighbors, use increasingly strident rhetoric in defense of China's national interests, and take a tougher line in relations with the United States and its allies to shift public focus away from economic troubles. He may also turn to greater economic protectionism.

These changes come at a time when Xi's tight control of the decision-making process has made it harder for U.S. policymakers to anticipate China's next moves. Familiar interlocutors at the State Council and Foreign Ministry, who once provided much-needed insight into an often mysterious policymaking process, are no longer central within it.

As the shroud of secrecy surrounding Chinese decision-making thick-ens, what remains clear is that dealing with China will require a more nuanced understanding of the man with singular control over the coun-try's foreign policy future. It will also necessitate an appreciation of the interaction between his internal political requirements and his foreign policy agenda. Finally, it will demand a clear-eyed acceptance of the fact that Xi has ushered in a new era of Chinese regional and global diplo-macy, one that will push the West to evaluate its overall approach to the People's Republic of China (PRC) and to the powerful but exposed leader who makes its foreign policy.

A System Transformed: Xi's Consolidation of Political Power

Xi has fundamentally changed the systems of Chinese governance. Under the preceding model, previous generations of Chinese leaders since Deng Xiaoping created a structure that embedded leadership and decision-making within a collective system of checks and balances that spanned a variety of bureaucratic institutions and included a substantial number of party elites. This consensus-driven system, forged in the wake of the tragic and devastating Cultural Revolution, shunned Maoist cults of personality and embraced the studied staidness of leaders like Hu Jintao.[4]

These bureaucratic procedures and prerogatives no longer function as before. Xi has introduced a new system by limiting collective leadership and marginalizing the traditional institutions of governance, relying instead on a small coterie of close advisors and an array of parallel structures to control policymaking.[5] These structures take the form of "leading small groups," which have long been part of China's governance, but appear now to be proliferating in number, growing in importance, and increasingly operational rather than strategic.[6] They are often chaired by Xi and staffed by loyal colleagues. The National Security Commission created in 2013, for example, is led by two figures who are close to Xi but hail from the provinces and have little foreign policy experience.[7] Such groups not only formulate and implement policy but also inform it, producing policy papers and ad hoc briefings tailored for Xi that have greater influence than those dutifully prepared by the ministries. As a direct result, senior officials are often unaware of policy being developed both at higher levels and in other parts of the system. With respect to foreign policy, Xi has reduced the role of the State Council, Foreign Ministry, and military in important decisions. These centralizing actions have given him greater freedom from governmental machinery and the political and bureaucratic opponents that can influence Chinese foreign policy.

Xi has been able to achieve this dramatic transformation by amassing power quickly, in part through his unprecedented campaign against corruption. This has also on occasion spurred surprises among the senior ranks of the Chinese government. Xi's right-hand advisor and fellow standing committee member, Wang Qishan, has for the moment used the campaign to silence potential opponents within the party. The arrest and prosecution of Zhou Yongkang, a former standing committee member, made clear that even the highest-level party elites are not safe from the anticorruption inquiry, especially given that many have themselves taken part in financial improprieties.[8]

Xi has likewise targeted the military and reversed the growing autonomy of the People's Liberation Army (PLA). His arrest of Vice Chairman of the Central Military Commission Xu Caihou for selling promotions suggests that dozens of generals who purchased their ranks are at risk of imprisonment.[9] In addition to intimidating military elites, Xi has created an atmosphere of uncertainty by questioning the PLA's operational readiness while pointing to a variety of looming foreign threats, which together justify reform and the party's guiding hand.[10] Finally, Xi has stressed on dozens of occasions that the PLA must remain an armed wing of the Chinese Communist Party (CCP). This was most apparent in his decision to call a meeting of hundreds of generals and military officials in Gutian County, the historic site where Mao Zedong first declared that the military must always be loyal to the party.[11] Together, Xi's efforts send an unmistakable signal to the PLA that compliance is expected and resistance punished.

Xi's arrest of senior officials is risky, and is sustained in no small part by public opinion supportive of the anticorruption campaign and of Xi more broadly. Unlike recent Chinese leaders, Xi appears to have an intuitive grasp of public sentiment and has sustained a nascent cult of personality around his image as a brash and assertive strongman, reportedly telling Russian President Vladimir Putin in 2013, "We are similar in character."[12] This image is buttressed by a relentless propaganda campaign waged through traditional and social media that portrays Xi as an incorruptible and self-sacrificial "mix of everyman and superman."[13] That effort has been successful in making public opinion a pillar of Xi's power, with a Harvard study finding that Xi had a higher approval rating domestically than any other world leader in 2014.[14]

Understanding the Man at the Center: Xi's Background and Biases

Because of Xi's unprecedented power and influence, Chinese policy will increasingly be determined by his background and biases—and therefore will be significantly more unpredictable. Although lacking a direct window into Xi's tight-knit decision-making structures, Westerners now know more about Xi himself.

Xi is the son of a revolutionary who fought alongside Mao. He reportedly sees himself and his fellow "princelings" as tasked with rescuing and reviving the Communist Party, to which he is dedicated. Like others who have longtime family ties to the party, Xi is said to be skeptical of the loyalty of those "hired hands" who have muscled their way to the top of the party hierarchy on the strength of merit and educational pedigree but whose fathers never bled for the revolution.[15]

Xi's dedication to the Chinese Communist Party shapes his views on what he perceives as two of the largest threats to its longevity: corruption and liberalism. Xi has long had a deep-seated disdain for the decadence and corruption of party officials, whose greed threatens the party's public support. He is deeply suspicious of Western values and intentions, and especially concerned about possible parallels with the Soviet Union's collapse. He has personally commissioned studies on that subject and forced cadres to watch documentaries on the dangers of Western cultural influence.[16] Xi's arrest of more than two hundred thousand party officials under the anticorruption campaign is one product of these beliefs; so too is his detention of thousands of lawyers and civil society leaders, the most in nearly two decades. Reinforced by Putin, Xi sees the hidden hand of Western forces behind China's domestic disturbances, including in Hong Kong, and these prejudices contribute to a profound distrust of the West that will be close to impossible to overcome.

Temperamentally, Xi is self-confident and keeps his own counsel. His willingness to take risks in his domestic and foreign policy was presaged by the early days of his career, when he relinquished the safety and comfort of a senior position in Beijing for a mid-level post in rural Hebei that he hoped would give him practical governing experience.[17] Unlike previous Chinese leaders, Xi frequently deviates from his talking points in meetings with foreign officials. Some Chinese officials suggest that Xi—although he has been guarded and strategic for much of his life—is occasionally impatient and impetuous, and that he at times makes decisions rashly. In short, this is a portrait of a complex and ambitious man at the pinnacle of power.

Powerful but Exposed: Xi in the Wake of China's Economic Slowdown

Xi is exposed precisely because he sits at the center of all decision-making and is visible to the public. He must address countless domestic challenges for which he is now explicitly accountable, and a major misstep on any of them could be costly to his political popularity and position. Without question, the largest problem looming over Xi's tenure is China's economic slowdown and its related manifestations, including unemployment and stock market volatility. As noted, China's economy, which had expanded at an annual rate of 10 percent for three decades, is entering a new era of slow growth that has forced the government to reduce its growth target to a record-low 6.5 percent. Xi's challenge is to smoothly reorient the economy toward consumption and away from exports and investment even as growth continues to fall.

China's economic woes began years before Xi entered the presidency and flow from the country's inability to find a sustainable alternative to the growth model upon which it has long relied. That model, which catapulted the country into the ranks of great powers, was based on a simple premise: weak-productivity agricultural laborers would move into low-wage but high-productivity manufacturing jobs, producing goods for foreign markets. Nearly every component of that model has been subject to mounting strain. China has fewer agricultural workers that it can shift into industry. Its workforce peaked in 2013 and is now shrinking in size.[18] Its wages often exceed those of regional competitors even as productivity growth slows.[19] Finally, China's export markets can no longer soak up its surplus production.

After the 2008 global financial crisis, China began to cope with these vulnerabilities using a mixture of cheap lending and massive infrastructure investment. For a time, this investment-heavy approach was able to return China to high growth, but it was not sustainable. Investment now accounts for roughly half of Chinese growth, an unprecedentedly high amount, and it is subject to diminishing returns, with one dollar of investment producing 40 percent less GDP growth today than it did a decade ago.[20] Meanwhile, the loans that underwrite these unproductive investments—such as China's famed ghost cities, which are filled with buildings but lacking in tenants or businesses—threaten the country's banking system and have pushed debt to 280 percent of GDP, according to a recent estimate from McKinsey & Company.[21] A significant portion of these loans, and by some accounts a majority, have been disbursed to inefficient state-owned enterprises (SOEs) rather than to productive private-sector companies, which in any case face higher interest rates than state companies. If these loans to SOEs are not paid back, they will threaten the banking system and the overall economy.[22] Growth having slowed every year since 2010, the party is under pressure to continue rebalancing the economy away from exports and investment and toward consumption, and to do so without systemic disruption.

The sudden decline in the Chinese stock market in the summer of 2015 and again in January 2016 raised worries in China and around the world that the party, under Xi, will fail to make this structurally difficult transition. These concerns are compounded by widespread distrust of official statistics and the belief of some economists that a hard landing may already be under way. At the peak of the crisis, the market decline wiped out trillions of dollars in wealth and temporarily reversed many of the gains of the preceding year. This was a considerable setback, but it is important not to overstate its significance for the finances of most Chinese citizens and the state of the economy. Less than a fifth of household wealth is in stocks, and much more of it is invested in a property market that has remained stable throughout the stock market's recent swings. Moreover, the stock market has a tradeable value less than a third of China's economy, compared with more than 100 percent in developed countries.[23]

The real risk to China's economy, and to Xi's fortunes, comes not from the stock market's raw economic impact but from the damage done to the government's credibility. Xi's strongman image suffered in the wake of the market collapse. His government had vocally encouraged average Chinese citizens to enter the country's stock market under the premise that good returns would incentivize higher spending, and was embarrassed when those investors were singed by the crash.[24] The government then publicly staked its credibility on a commitment to arrest the stock market decline, but its ill-conceived market manipulations and hasty currency devaluations were of limited effectiveness. Eventually,

China was able to reverse the declines, but similar or repeated episodes will undermine the party's legitimacy.

Aside from the perceptual costs posed by such economic downturns, Xi faces the considerable risk that a prolonged slowdown will directly affect the welfare of the average Chinese citizen. The possibility of a hard landing looms, and an economic wreck or a serious financial crisis could produce years of prolonged stagnation and slow growth that could shake the party to its core. Even absent such a disaster, if growth continues to slow, it will worsen a number of internal trends. The labor market already struggles to absorb the eight million college graduates China's universities produce each year. Blue-collar wages that had risen for a decade have been stagnant for well over a year as layoffs continue in coastal factories, with labor disputes doubling in 2014 and again in 2015.[25]

Chinese companies also face challenges, as corporate debt grows to 160 percent of China's GDP, up from 98 percent in 2008 and more than twice the current U.S. level of 70 percent. The fragile recovery in the country's property market could face a reversal that would undercut what is the biggest store of household wealth for Chinese families. These problems could intertwine with the psychic impact of another stock market swing or economic crisis, which could further erode consumer confidence and jeopardize China's economic reorientation.[26] Business and investor trust have similarly been hit, largely because the government's panicked attempts to control the market signaled the hesitancy of its commitment to reform. If the government's reputation is diminished and economic growth remains stagnant, then the leadership will grow increasingly worried about social unrest. Past economic crises contributed to outbreaks of mass protests, including those in 1986 and 1989 that brought down two Chinese leaders, Hu Yaobang and Zhao Ziyang, and led to the violence in Tiananmen Square. Although the party weathered the stock market slumps reasonably well, there is no guarantee it will be so fortunate in a future crisis.

The reputational challenges and economic obstacles Xi faces will not abate in the next few years. Removing them will require implementing a number of costly reforms to inefficient SOEs, providing affordable capital to the private sector, allowing workers greater geographic mobility, reducing inefficient forms of infrastructure investment, and building the commercial rule of law. These inherently disruptive moves would break China's old growth model but could risk increased social instability, leaving Xi struggling to choose between high-quality growth tomorrow and societal order today. If Xi largely abandons reforms and doubles down on the current model, he will only delay the day of reckoning; if he pursues reforms, it could take years before he sees results. Regardless of which course he chooses, or if he tries to square the circle, China's economy will likely slow for the next few years and the reputational risks to Xi will continue to rise as domestic frustrations mount.

Some analysts are skeptical that the situation is quite so serious. In their more sanguine view, economies naturally slow as they get bigger and China's economy is already twice as large as it was seven years ago. Mathematically, this means that even if growth slows to half its previous pace, it will still generate income gains that are just as large in absolute terms. This fact, however, by no means guarantees political stability. Even if some Western economists believe that 5 percent growth is healthy, that is no guarantee or even likelihood that Chinese citizens or Chinese elites will agree. First, the distribution of China's economic growth matters enormously. Given China's exceptional and widening inequality, the benefits of economic growth do not easily benefit the average citizen. Second, citizens who have known rapid income growth for their entire working lives will be disappointed at the slowdown—especially if it leads to layoffs and higher unemployment that actually worsen the average quality of life. Signs of unrest already abound, with labor disputes and "mass incidents" on the rise, as noted earlier.[27] Finally, widespread corruption, environmental degradation, pervasive societal inequality, and repressive autocracy are more palatable when incomes are climbing quickly; when they are not, these simmering issues can boil over into protest. Senior Chinese leaders clearly think in such terms, many—including former Premier Wen Jiabao—having previously stated that 8 percent growth is needed to maintain social stability.[28] Such growth is no longer attainable, and at a senior conclave of top Chinese economic officials held in December 2015, many acknowledged the possibility of stagnant growth for years to come.[29]

The impact of this situation on Xi's political position is evolving. For now, Xi remains strong, his opposition is divided, and nothing indicates that his leadership is in jeopardy. Media reports suggest, however, that senior party members were alarmed by the gyrations of the stock market in the summer of 2015 and the country's sputtering growth and are holding Xi accountable. They are encouraging him to focus more on the economic situation than the anticorruption campaign, which some

contend slows growth by paralyzing rank-and-file officials who fear that
action on new projects could land them in jail.[30] If the economy continues to weaken, party elites who have suffered under the anticorruption campaign may seek to exploit the situation to undermine Xi, who
now has the dubious distinction of presiding over the slowest growth
in thirty years and whose agenda and image are underwritten by public
support that could wane.

Xi will need to take clear steps to strengthen his position against rival
elites, fortify his public image, and shield the party from the economic
downturn. To that end, he will probably intensify his personality cult,
crack down even harder on dissent, and grow bolder in using the anticorruption campaign against elites who oppose him. Above all, he will
almost certainly choose to intensify and stimulate Chinese nationalism
in response to slower growth. Ever since Deng dispatched communist
ideology in favor of pragmatic capitalist reforms, the party's legitimacy
has been built on two pillars: economic growth and nationalist ideology. Because the former is fading, the latter may be the primary tool to
support the edifice of the party and Xi's strongman image.

The foundations for a turn to nationalism have been laid for decades.
After Tiananmen Square, the party inculcated nationalist sentiment
through relentless propaganda, a barrage of chauvinistic television
shows and movies, and a "patriotic education campaign" in the country's schools.[31] According to the government's nationalist narrative,
which downplays the party's failures and communist ideology, China is
a country whose "century of humiliation" began with the Opium Wars
and ended with the party's assumption of power in 1949. The party's
primary mission has not been to bring about a communist utopia but
to extricate China from the predations of Western and Japanese impe-
rialists and to put it on a path to becoming the world's largest economy.
China's territorial disputes with its neighbors and Taiwan's ambiguous
status are seen as wounds from this humiliating past that only the party
can heal.

This slanted view of history has been successful in building a deep
reserve of grievance and victimhood among ordinary Chinese citizens
that dominates their worldview and can be harnessed by the leadership.
It was no accident that Xi, when he assumed power, declared that his
main objective was to bring about the "great rejuvenation of the Chinese nation." That slogan was an attempt to position Xi's leadership
within the arc of a larger narrative that portrays the party as responsible

for restoring China's historic place in the world. In December 2015, the Communist Party Central Committee held a group study of Chinese patriotism and Xi himself called for further "promoting patriotism to achieve the great rejuvenation of the Chinese nation."[32] By connecting patriotism to Xi's mission to restore Chinese greatness, that link is being made even more concrete.

Although these themes have long been an important part of Chinese politics, Xi will choose to strengthen them in coming years. By stoking Chinese nationalism, Xi will seek to protect himself and the party from the worst of the economic downturn. His control over policymaking will be an advantage in that effort, and his policies will reflect and support his domestic political agenda.

A Mix of Bullying and Beneficence: Xi's Current Foreign Policy

Xi's foreign policy to date has been conducted free from the reality of a prolonged lower-growth trajectory. An analysis of that foreign policy, which bears his imprimatur, is necessary before speculating about its future direction in the wake of China's unfolding economic retrenchment.

Xi's transformation of China's domestic politics has ushered in a new era in the country's external behavior, but the break from previous foreign policy, though significant, is not as dramatic as some might assume. Xi has taken pains to highlight his departure from what he regards as the weak policies of the enfeebled Hu administration. In many cases, however, Xi's policies and strategic objectives exhibit continuity with those of the last few years of his predecessor's tenure, which saw increased assertiveness on territorial matters in the East China Sea, South China Sea, and Indian border, as well as the use of coercive geoeconomic tools against others and strident objections to U.S. power projection into the region.

What sets Xi's foreign policy apart the most is his willingness to use every instrument of statecraft, from military assets to geoeconomic intimidation, as well as explicit economic rewards, to pursue his various geopolitical objectives. Although China has used geoeconomic instruments for more than fifteen years, the current leadership controls more wealth than any other government in Chinese history and exhibits a greater willingness to use it in an assertive, nuanced, and diversified way to simultaneously induce cooperation and penalize recalcitrance.[33] In general, Xi's policy has been characterized by bullying over territorial issues and selective beneficence on economic matters, with the looming application of economic coercion ever present. His ability to implement such a policy has been facilitated by his centralization of policymaking. This has allowed him to act in a quick and coordinated fashion across policy domains and to retreat from Deng's admonition to keep a low profile, facilitating the nimble and synchronized deployment of rewards and punishments to China's neighbors.

This approach has been clearest in China's relations with Southeast Asian states, many of which are embroiled in a simmering territorial dispute with Beijing over the South China Sea. China has so far refrained from seizing additional islands; nevertheless, it has been much more assertive with the other claimants to the South China Sea. China unilaterally deployed an oil rig to the Spratly Islands, only 120 miles from Vietnam's coast, and reportedly sent eighty vessels to protect it.[34] Chinese coast guard vessels have harassed Filipino and Vietnamese fishing boats and anchored in Malaysia's exclusive economic zone (EEZ).[35] In less than two years, China has also reclaimed seventeen times more land in the South China Sea than all other claimants combined over the past forty years. China's additions account for 95 percent of total reclaimed land and more than 2,900 acres in all, some of which is now home to runways and mobile artillery.[36] Even small fishing boats receive instructions from Beijing, never mind the dredging vessels and state oil companies, indicating that these tough policies are the result of intentional and coordinated action rather than the sum of diverse bureaucratic forces acting independently.[37]

Beijing's hardening position on these territorial disputes has been accompanied by generous investment and trade packages to Southeast Asian states, and these too appear to be coordinated centrally to geopolitical ends. In 2014, China pledged more than $20 billion in aid to Southeast Asian states. AIIB and Beijing's One Belt, One Road initiative, which would provide tens of billions of dollars more in infrastructure financing to that region, have been the focus of a working group personally led by Xi, who himself announced the initiatives during a visit to Southeast Asia.[38] That these reassuring gestures have come in the midst of China's aggressive moves in the South China Sea suggests that China seeks to demonstrate the benefits of cooperation against the stark backdrop of potential conflict.

A mixture of hard and soft policies has likewise characterized China's relations with India. During Xi's first visit to India, Chinese troops launched one of their largest incursions ever into disputed territory with India. Whether the move was deliberate or incidental is a subject of some debate, but it was nonetheless regarded as menacing in New Delhi, which has noted a sharp uptick in Chinese border violations in recent years. China has sought to use the border to keep India off balance and reduce its maritime military investments, which is at least one reason Beijing has been unwilling to delineate the Line of Actual Control (LAC) despite Indian Prime Minster Narendra Modi's public request that the two countries do so. An agreement on the LAC would set the stage for a compromise and reduce the possibility of accidental conflict.

Beijing's uncompromising positions on the border have been accompanied by offers of lavish aid for Indian infrastructure and increased investment in Indian companies. When Xi visited in 2014, he pledged to help India modernize its railway system, establish high-speed rail in India, build industrial parks in Gujarat and Maharashtra, and expand market access for select Indian goods. He also pledged $20 billion in aid over five years.[39] Importantly, China invited India to join the AIIB as a founding member, where it will likely be the second-largest state by vote share, and which opens the possibility that New Delhi could secure billions more in infrastructure assistance. Together, these economic overtures are aimed at inducing closer cooperation with India and giving India a substantial economic stake in good relations with Beijing. China has also increased its diplomacy in the rest of South Asia, offering Pakistan $46 billion in new aid, dispatching nuclear submarines to Sri Lanka, selling arms to Indian neighbors such as Bangladesh, and even providing eight new submarines to Pakistan to help it offset India's naval advantage—all of which puts pressure on Indian security and strengthens China's in the region.[40]

With respect to Japan, China has pursued a tough and nationalistic policy. Under Xi, China has dramatically escalated its territorial dispute with Japan through its declaration of an Air Defense Identification Zone (ADIZ) in the East China Sea. It has staged repeat incursions by aircraft and coast guard vessels into Japanese territory surrounding the Senkaku/Diaoyu Islands and built oil and gas platforms close to them. Chinese military officials and academics have begun to question Japanese sovereignty over Okinawa, and Foreign Ministry spokeswoman Hua Chunying demurred when asked whether Okinawa is part of Japan.[41] China began toughening its position under Hu, who reduced rare-earth exports to Japan during a crisis over the Senkaku/Diaoyu Islands, and it has not made any serious attempt at reassurance under Xi. The only potential bright spot is the China-Japan-South Korea Free

Trade Agreement (FTA), as well as a successful trilateral leader-level summit between these countries in November 2015, but substantive progress remains limited in the wake of these territorial disputes.

Xi's foreign policy is not only balanced across hard and soft tools of statecraft but also diversified across its bilateral targets. Xi has pursued an omnidirectional foreign policy that also emphasizes ties with European Union (EU) members, Brazil, South Africa, and especially Russia. The levying of Western sanctions against Russia following its invasion of Ukraine drove Moscow and Beijing closer together. The two countries struck intensified deals on energy and weapons, conducted joint military exercises in far-flung theaters, and signed a historic pact on cybersecurity committing each side to refrain from hacking the other. Signs now point to even greater coordination on Asian affairs following their first bilateral meeting dedicated exclusively to the region's security matters.

Aside from developing stronger ties with other states, an important element of Xi's multifaceted strategy has been to energetically create and participate in multilateral institutions. Some of these, such as AIIB, will be useful for dispensing geoeconomically oriented loans to neighbors. Even though AIIB is a multilateral lending institution rather than a Chinese government agency, such organizations can still be used for geoeconomic statecraft, especially given that Beijing will retain significant influence in AIIB's management and operation as well as a veto. For example, China sought to use the Asian Development Bank to deny loans to Arunachal Pradesh, an Indian state claimed by China. The misguided refusal of the United States to participate in the AIIB's creation, and Washington's failed attempt to persuade friends and allies not to join, denied the United States an opportunity to influence the bank's rules, development trajectory, and China's potential use of the bank as a geopolitical instrument.

Other organizations in which China has been dominant have served to exclude the United States from regional discussions or provided China a forum that parallels and circumvents global institutions, allowing it to pursue its national interests and attempt to reshape global governance. China's elevation of the Conference on Interaction and Confidence-Building Measures in Asia (CICA), a forum that does not include the United States, gave Xi the opportunity to advocate an "Asia for Asians" and amplify long-standing criticism of U.S. bilateral alliances. Its creation of the New Development Bank (formerly the BRICS—Brazil,

Russia, India, China, and South Africa—Development Bank) and the Regional Comprehensive Economic Partnership (RCEP) parallels the World Bank and the Trans-Pacific Partnership (TPP) and offers it the ability to wield geoeconomic influence over others. Although many of these initiatives were conceived under Hu, they were given life by Xi. Because China has historically been hesitant to create and lead multilateral initiatives, this self-assured and multidirectional Chinese behavior is yet another example of increased activism related to Xi's rise.

Xi's decisive leadership style, his unmatched power within the political system, and his strong desire for vigorous Chinese diplomacy have produced a foreign policy that is assertive, coordinated, and diversified across the instruments and targets of statecraft.

Xi's September 2015 State Visit to the United States

The summit between President Barack Obama and President Xi was a high-stakes affair. Both countries turned to the bilateral meeting after a period of focus on other matters, with the United States busy on the Iran nuclear agreement and China coping with one of its most intense macroeconomic crises in decades. The atmospherics surrounding the summit were complex and controversial. The United States was preparing sanctions on Chinese entities involved in the cyber-enabled theft of intellectual property, and China had just concluded a military rally in Tiananmen Square that overtly featured its "carrier-killing" antiship ballistic missile. Xi's arrival in Washington was also preceded by the first operation of Chinese warships in U.S. territorial waters off the Alaskan coast, evoking memories of Cold War encounters between U.S. and Soviet forces in the same area.

Coming at a time of deepening distrust between the United States and China, especially on issues related to freedom of navigation and cyber hacking, the summit was arguably one of the most important meetings between an American and Chinese leader in recent memory. The highly choreographed visit went as well as could be expected and was not without minor accomplishment. Both sides signed an agreement limiting cyber theft and promised to refrain from hacking critical infrastructure in peacetime, though it remains to be seen whether China will cease and desist. They also agreed on a joint statement for combating climate change. Yet, on a variety of other issues, especially the territorial disputes in the South China Sea, the visit produced no substantive progress.

For Xi, the meeting was as much an exercise in public messaging and image-making as an attempt at finding agreements on policy, and perhaps the greatest progress came on climate change. Xi's announcement of a cap-and-trade program by 2017 positioned China ahead of the international curve on climate change before the United Nations (UN) climate change conference in Paris. These efforts followed a precedent-setting though nonbinding 2014 agreement between the United States and China that committed the United States to reduce emissions 26 to 28 percent below 2005 levels by 2025 and required China to peak carbon emissions by 2030. These two bilateral agreements laid the foundation for a breakthrough agreement at the Paris climate summit in December 2015 that, for the first time, committed every country to lower greenhouse gas emissions. That China played such a large part in facilitating the Paris agreement redounded to Xi Jinping's domestic and foreign leadership and image.

In addition to new initiatives on climate change, Xi also committed $1 billion and eight thousand peacekeepers to the United Nations during his U.S. visit, suggesting a newfound willingness to shoulder greater international responsibility. Xi also promised not to militarize new islands in the South China Sea, as the PRC has been doing; welcomed nongovernmental organizations (NGOs), on which China has been systematically cracking down; and praised women's rights, which are hardly a strength of the CCP regime.

But nowhere was Xi's attempt at messaging clearer than in his decision to begin his U.S. visit in Seattle. Aware that Obama was likely to threaten China with sanctions over cyber hacking, Xi departed from the usual stage-managed script of state visits and called for a meeting of U.S. technology company chief executive officers (CEOs) at Microsoft's headquarters. By doing so, he sought to preempt Obama's criticism and the possibility of U.S. sanctions by appearing to constructively work with U.S. companies, all the while signaling Chinese economic power with his ability to summon the CEOs of so many prominent American firms.[42] In a similar demonstration of China's geoeconomic reach, he also announced in Seattle a major purchase of Boeing passenger aircraft.[43]

As Obama has stressed, in light of all Xi's initiatives and promises, "The question now is, 'Are words followed by actions?'" Xi's reassuring message to U.S. technology companies means little when so many of them are banned or under investigation in China. He may yet renege on promises to refrain from hacking critical infrastructure or stealing foreign technology—indeed, by some reports China has already broken its recent cyber agreement with the United States—and the details of his climate cap-and-trade program remain vague.[44] Xi's promise not to militarize South China Sea islands appears empty given his decision to construct airstrips and docks—and place artillery—on those islands. Similarly, Xi's praise for women's rights and his remarks welcoming NGOs stand at odds with his detention of feminist activists and his promulgation of a law that will close many NGOs operating in China.[45] Observers will be watching not only whether Xi honors his summit commitments, but also what the United States does in the aftermath of the summit with respect to freedom of navigation and other issues that have been in contention between the two countries.

In any case, there is little reason to believe that Xi's words will fundamentally improve the tone or substance of the bilateral relationship. The primary purpose of Xi's trip was to enhance his prestige and modestly reassure the United States at a time of souring business and U.S. domestic opinion, all the while refusing to compromise on significant Chinese national interests. Although it remains unclear whether he has achieved this goal, at least one conclusion seems firm enough: Xi's visit, and especially his meeting in Seattle with technology CEOs, is strong evidence of his ability to react nimbly and effectively to U.S. initiatives and demonstrates his gift for public relations. In this regard, it showcases the nature of the challenge that U.S. policymakers face in dealing with him in the future.

Diplomacy After the Downturn: Xi's Future Foreign Policy

Economic growth and nationalism have for decades been the two founts of legitimacy for the Communist Party, and as the former wanes, Xi will likely rely increasingly on the latter. Since 1989, the party has deliberately and carefully laid the foundation for such a strategy through patriotic education, censorship, government-backed protests against Japan, and relentless news and popular media that have reinforced a nationalist victimization narrative.

As a powerful but exposed leader, Xi will tap into this potent nationalist vein through foreign policy, burnishing his nationalist credentials and securing his domestic position from elite and popular criticism, all while pursuing various Chinese national interests. For example, an emphasis on territorial disputes and historical grievances could partially divert attention from the country's economic woes and arrest a potential decline in his public approval; in contrast, a visible setback or controversial concession on such issues could undermine his standing with Chinese citizens and party elites. On economic matters, concerns over growth and employment may lead China to become increasingly recalcitrant and self-interested.

In the future, Xi could become more hostile to the West, using it as a foil to boost his approval ratings the way Putin has in Russia. Already, major Chinese newspapers are running articles blaming the country's economic slump on efforts undertaken by insidious "foreign forces" that seek to sabotage the country's rise. Even if Xi does not seek more combative relations with the West, he will nonetheless find it difficult to negotiate publicly on a variety of issues, especially when nationalist sentiment runs high.

On territorial matters, Xi will be unwilling or unable to make concessions that could harm his domestic position, and may even seek to escalate territorial disputes against Japan or South China Sea claimants as a way of redirecting domestic attention away from the economic situation and burnishing his nationalist record. A dangerous but unlikely possibility is that Xi may even be tempted to use military force to instigate limited conflicts against the Philippines, Vietnam, or Japan. Given that Japan is a prominent target of China's propaganda and media, and that memories of Japan's brutal occupation are still influential, ties between China and Japan may continue to worsen.

Xi entered office suggesting that he would not alter China's policies toward Taiwan, but that may change following the election of Democratic Progressive Party (DPP) candidate Tsai Ing-wen in January 2016. The DPP has historically been distant toward China, and though it has moderated its pro-independence stance, its leaders remain opponents of current President Ma Ying-jeou's efforts to strengthen economic links with China, skeptics of the 1992 consensus, and critical of the historic meeting between Presidents Xi and Ma in November 2015. Xi's unbending stance on sovereignty and territorial integrity, combined with the real domestic political costs he will face if Taiwan makes moves toward independence, may lead him to react strongly and decisively to any Taiwanese policy under the DPP that is designed to increase separation between Beijing and Taipei.[46]

With respect to North Korea, it appears unlikely that Xi Jinping's more assertive foreign policy will lead him to exert meaningful pressure on the oppressive communist regime. Xi's approach has been harsher toward North Korea than that of his predecessors, with Xi refraining from making a traditional state visit to North Korea, restricting exports of weapons-related materials and chemicals, cutting ties with some North Korean banks, and publicly reprimanding the regime for threatening regional security.[47] This toughness, however, apparently has limits. Even after North Korea's January 2016 nuclear test, China has remained unwilling to use its considerable leverage over Pyongyang—which depends on China for food and fuel—to change North Korean behavior. In China's view, crippling cuts to North Korea's supply of oil and food would risk chaos in the North, and perhaps even a collapse that could result in a united Korea that is a U.S. treaty ally. Globally, Xi will maintain a proactive and assertive Chinese foreign policy that involves institution-building and occasional provocation in order to demonstrate at home that China is taken seriously abroad. Xi will remain firm in the face of external pressure on the South and East China Seas, human rights, conditions in Tibet and Xinjiang, and diplomatic visits by the Dalai Lama. As China assumes the rotating presidency of the

Group of Twenty (G20), Xi will continue to challenge the U.S. global financial and security order using institutional methods.

China's economic woes may also influence Xi's foreign policy in ways unrelated to nationalism. Although it is possible that China could scale back costly aid and development programs, such as the One Belt, One Road initiative and AIIB, this will probably not occur. China has more than $3.5 trillion in foreign reserves, and these programs would require it to deploy only a fraction of that amount in the form of loans and grants. In addition to that spent on China's geopolitical objectives, much of this aid will go to infrastructure projects that will contract Chinese companies for construction materials, labor, and engineering, and therefore serve as a way of compensating for reduced domestic investment.

The slowdown may, however, lead China to become marginally more protectionist and mercantile, especially if such efforts are thought to boost employment and thereby enhance social stability. Never totally committed to markets or free trade, China could close some labor-intensive industries, further devalue its currency, be uncooperative on intellectual property theft, and step up its harassment of foreign businesses. For the most part, however, its protectionist impulses will be restrained by its obligations to the World Trade Organization (WTO) and its need for foreign capital and markets. In his deals with foreign commodity suppliers, including Russia, Xi will insist on more advantageous terms and be less inclined to grant debt forgiveness to Ecuador and Venezuela, which currently repay Chinese loans with oil. Although Xi could attempt to use China's economic woes to justify further reforms and commit to market mechanisms, the record so far suggests that he is willing to sacrifice that agenda in an attempt to regain short-term growth and maintain employment. To cope with the stock market slide, for example, Xi rolled out a slew of initiatives that reversed capital market liberalization and financial reforms.

China will continue to limit its responsibilities in global governance, preferring instead shallow commitments.[48] This will be particularly the case in global institutions where China does not play a rule-making role. The leadership, long hesitant to take action on such matters, may now feel less equipped to do so. As China's economy slows, Xi will not be willing to agree to binding or inflexible environmental initiatives to combat climate change, especially if they would further weaken the country's fragile economy. Global economic management in organizations such as the G20 may also become problematic, China being possibly less inclined to act responsibly on economic matters.

Finally, Xi's resistance to Western culture and values may intensify. Xi has arrested countless dissidents, civil society leaders, and activists; sharply curtailed the ability of NGOs to operate; intensified controls over the media and the Internet; and inveighed against Western cultural contamination while extolling Confucianism. Because China's economy is now slowing, Xi's fear of political instability may push him to adopt even sterner measures, and new violations of human rights and the emerging challenges that Western NGOs and businesses face will likely cause renewed friction in China's relationships with the West.

Implications for the United States

The U.S.-China bilateral relationship is the most important in the world. No other two countries under foreseeable circumstances could disrupt the international system. Thus, Xi Jinping's rise, his dominance of China's policymaking process, and the increasing influence of his domestic political concerns will have crucial consequences for the United States and for American policies in Asia and beyond.

Although China's relationship with the United States has long been a priority for Chinese leaders, Xi has increasingly been willing to test it and it occupies less of his attention than it did of his predecessors'. He has not only criticized U.S. alliances, questioned the role of non-Asian powers in Asian affairs, and built alternative institutional structures excluding the United States, but has also continued China's rapid military modernization even as the Chinese economy slows. As China asserts its vital national interests, one of which is limiting the U.S. role in Asian affairs and related power projection capabilities, Beijing's positions on matters ranging from the U.S. alliance system in Asia, to freedom of navigation, to human rights, to the territorial integrity of Japan, to the rise of India, to the future of Taiwan will come into sustained tension with U.S. national interests, policies, commitments, and values.

Nevertheless, China's growing geopolitical ambitions are tempered by the reality of its economic relationship with the United States and a variety of shared international interests between the two countries. China will continue to seek to expand its influence and in some instances will compete directly with the United States, and Xi may criticize Washington to score points at home, but bilateral economic interdependence will, in most cases, provide a floor for the relationship. This is, of course, different from the longtime U.S. objective of constraining and ultimately moderating Chinese behavior by broadly integrating China into the international system, a strategy that appears not to have substantially shaped China's more assertive external policies. In sum, Xi does not want to trigger a confrontation with the United States, especially during a period of economic uncertainty in China.

Nevertheless, U.S. policymakers will likely face a growing challenge in Xi, particularly because he can coordinate a variety of different instruments of statecraft in service of enduring Chinese strategic objectives and to bolster his nationalist credentials. By contrast, U.S. policymakers are burdened by a slower, more divided, and more public interagency process. Xi will exploit the relative opacity and speed of his system to keep U.S. officials off balance with new initiatives or provocations. These Chinese advantages are serious, but they are not necessarily decisive, especially if the United States remains resolved, strengthens its alliances, and forges a bipartisan domestic consensus on Asia policy.

To deal with Xi's more assertive foreign and defense policies, the United States should devise a grand strategy for Asia at least as coherent and coordinated as the one that has been formulated in Beijing, which appears designed to maximize China's power while challenging the long-standing role of the United States in the region.[49] What we have in mind is not containment, which in any case is a U.S.-Soviet concept that has no relevant application in East Asia today. Instead, the United States should use a variety of instruments of statecraft to incentivize China to commit to a rules-based order but impose costs that are in excess of the gains Beijing would reap if it fails to do so. This American grand strategy should account for the fact that the decades-long endeavor to integrate China into the global order has not significantly tempered China's strategic objective to become the most powerful and influential country in Asia. This being the case, the United States needs a long-term approach that demonstrates U.S. internal strength, external resolve, and steadiness of policy.

What we propose seeks to avoid a U.S.-China confrontation and maintain U.S. primacy in Asia. This will require a much more robust effort by Washington, together with its allies and friends in the region, to shape Chinese foreign policy—which may well become even more forceful as China's slowing economy calls into question political stability and induces the party to lean ever more on the pillar of popular nationalism to maintain legitimacy. Informed by Xi's unique stature and China's changed economic prospects, prescriptive suggestions for a U.S. strategy follow.

First, even as the Middle East and Europe once again call for attention, the United States should nevertheless continue its "pivot" or rebalance to Asia by strengthening its diplomatic, economic, and military ties across the region. Beijing recognizes that one of its great advantages in this strategic competition is how much time and attention Washington spends on challenges elsewhere. As China steps up its military challenge and its use of geoeconomic tools, the price of U.S. absence or hesitance in Asia has never been higher. A successful U.S. grand strategy should take as a given that economics and politics are profoundly intertwined in Asia and that Congress should pass the TPP if it is not to lose further strategic ground to China, as well as lift constraints on U.S. exports of oil and gas to its Asian allies.

Second, the United States should substantially strengthen its power projection into Asia. It should maintain commitments to deploy at least 60 percent of the U.S. Navy and Air Force to the region despite continuing crises in the Middle East and enduring challenges in Europe. The United States needs more frequent and formidable naval activities, more robust air force deployments, and more capable expeditionary formations, as well as greater partner capacity, to reinforce its preeminent role in preserving peace and stability in Asia. This will allow it not only to conduct freedom of navigation transits, but also to seek to deter Chinese provocations, respond to regional crises, and reassure allies. The October 2015 dispatch of a U.S. Navy warship to within twelve nautical miles of China's artificial islands in the South China Sea sent a powerful signal that the United States is determined to oppose China's assertions of sovereignty over international waters and to protect freedom of navigation. Such U.S. operations, including challenges to Beijing's unilaterally declared ADIZ, should be conducted as often as necessary to reinforce Asia's rules-based order and need not always be announced publicly before they are undertaken. For these types of operations to be effective, they will need to be consistent, which in turn requires a long-term military strategy that prioritizes the Asia-Pacific and commits to the region a level of military assets that reflects its foremost importance to U.S. national interests.

Third, even as China's behavior in Asia becomes increasingly provocative, the United States should refrain from seeking to implement a China-first approach to the region. Such a G-2 bilateral focus, including the signing of a "fourth communique" for U.S.-China relations, would suggest a great power condominium that puts China at the center of U.S. strategy in Asia. This would potentially raise the specter of a spheres of influence approach that would be contrary to the open and rules-based U.S. order and raise destabilizing concerns among U.S. allies and partners. Instead of pursuing a bilateral diplomatic grand bargain, Beijing's behavior is best influenced by a broad and coordinated American multilateral strategy that embraces and deepens diplomatic ties with states throughout the entire region, including China. In short, the United States should embed its China policy within a larger Asia-wide framework, intensifying every one of Washington's other bilateral relationships in the region. Deepening and diversifying contacts throughout Asia will allow the United States greater influence in the region's affairs and greater capacity to shape China's external choices.

Fourth, the United States should take the following steps in concert with its Asian allies and partners:

- *Japan.* The United States should continue to work with Japan to enhance the operational capabilities of the Japan Self-Defense Forces. In addition, the United States should upgrade its ballistic missile defense (BMD) cooperation with Japan, support Japan's cooperation with other Asian allies and partners, and regularly and resoundingly signal that the United States will come to Japan's defense if Japan is attacked.

- *South Korea.* The cornerstone of America's relationship with South Korea is their shared commitment to defending the latter from North Korean aggression. In that regard, the United States should promote stability on the Korean peninsula by maintaining enough military forces there to deter aggressive North Korean action, reaffirm its nuclear guarantees to South Korea, and enhance South Korea's BMD capabilities. Because China is acting consistently as the sole benefactor of South Korea's enemy to the north, it is crucial for the United States to uphold its status as the guarantor of stability on the Korean Peninsula, thus facilitating a shared vision of U.S.-South Korean national interests. The United States, South Korea, and Japan will together need to continue pushing China to use its leverage to restrain North Korea's nuclear ambitions, in part by reminding Beijing that North Korea's provocative behavior is a driving force behind defense modernization, exercises, and military deployments for the United States and its allies. Although it is unlikely that this allied diplomacy will produce any fundamental change in China's protective stance toward North Korea, Washington should keep trying.

- *Australia.* Australia is a linchpin of America's Indo-Pacific strategy. Canberra should host more, and more frequent, deployments of U.S. military assets in the region. The United States and Australia should greatly increase their cooperation on BMD, cybersecurity, intelligence gathering, and naval operations. Washington should support Canberra's diplomatic and military cooperation with other U.S. allies and partners in the region. The United States should also upgrade its free trade agreement with Australia and encourage it to enter into FTAs with other like-minded countries.

- *The Philippines.* On a visit to the Philippines in November 2015, President Barack Obama described the U.S. commitment to the Philippines' security as "ironclad," and emphasized that commitment by announcing the delivery of two U.S. ships to the navy of the Philippines.[50] Although this is a step in the right direction, the United States will need to redouble its efforts to help modernize the armed forces of the Philippines and enhance its operational capabilities if Manila is to ultimately have a role in deterring China from expanding its territorial claims.

- *India.* As the 2015 Council on Foreign Relations task force report on India noted, "India now matters to U.S. interests in virtually every dimension."[51] This is especially true in the Asia-Pacific, and the United States should improve ties with India by intensifying technology transfers, enhancing security cooperation, and inviting India into the Asia-Pacific Economic Cooperation forum. The United States should increase cooperation between the U.S. and Indian navies and continue to assist the Indian navy with modernization efforts to offset ambitious Chinese naval expansion. In addition, the United States should support Narendra Modi's Act East policy, meant to strengthen India's geoeconomic and power projection capabilities.

Although the PRC views increased U.S. coordination with its allies as a threat to its interests in the region, close ties and clear communication are important not only in dealing with common threats but also in reducing the likelihood that Asian allies take unnecessary risks with American support. Moreover, they permit the United States the opportunity to persuade or induce allies and partners not to rely exclusively on their bilateral relationship with the United States but also to increase cooperation and coordination with each other to build common security.[52]

Fifth, the United States should work with its Asian alliance members and other partners to devise a set of policies to deal with China's coercive geoeconomic policies. Currently, Beijing pays no price for using its economic instruments to pressure nations to acquiesce to its external objectives. Washington should immediately initiate a discussion with friendly Asian states to devise strategies designed to protect them from China's economic coercion and to diversify their economic options.[53] TPP is an important step in this direction, and support for the agreement from Congress would not only demonstrate U.S. staying power but also signal to China and our allies the depth of the long-term American commitment to the region's prosperity. Additional steps could include devising new multilateral institutions, free trade agreements, and investment agreements that can reduce the dependence of Asian nations on China as well as public condemnation of China's intimidating geoeconomic statecraft.

Sixth, because China's policymaking process will be opaque, unpredictable, and quick, U.S. officials need to meet even more often with the man who dominates it and his most senior colleagues. This is especially important in light of China's economic slowdown, which leaves the country's impenetrable domestic politics bound to play an even larger role in its external behavior. Leader-level dialogues involving Xi, such as the informal and open-collar summit between Obama and Xi at the Sunnylands estate in California, will become increasingly important in managing relations with China and learning the motivations and political concerns of its leader. That particular summit was a throwback to earlier days when President Richard Nixon and National Security Advisor Henry Kissinger met with Chinese leaders Mao Zedong and Zhou Enlai in Mao's living quarters, free from the scripted pageantry and prepared talking points of the usual state visit. U.S. officials will need more of these informal senior meetings in the future if they are to understand and influence Xi.

Seventh, the United States should marshal its diplomacy with nations within the region, as well as those outside it (e.g., European countries that favor rules-based approaches), to make progress on priorities such as free trade, regional security, and freedom of navigation. For example, public support for U.S. freedom of navigation operations in the South China Sea in October 2015 from countries including Australia and South Korea demonstrated that even states with deep economic ties to China will publicly advocate for widely held international norms.

An important reason the United States should consider such multilateral approaches is that Xi will likely have limited maneuvering room in public foreign policy crises, especially given China's downturn and Xi's likely need to intensify nationalist rhetoric and policy. These kinds of multilateral efforts can elevate what might otherwise appear to be a U.S. ideological criticism of Beijing to an appeal to respected international standards; in this way, such criticism may be less provocative and harmful to Xi's position than those applied in a purely bilateral fashion. Finally, although such public efforts have an important role in the prosecution of U.S. diplomacy toward China, the United States should also conduct private counsel with China—at least in the first instance—on issues that are especially sensitive.

Eighth, especially in a time of growing bilateral discord, the United States should intensify its overall diplomacy with Beijing. U.S.-China cooperation will pay dividends on a variety of global challenges and demonstrate to Asian states that the United States is doing whatever it can to avoid confrontation with China. Xi himself seems willing to collaborate on a number of issues. China has been involved in diplomacy aimed at constraining Iran's nuclear ambitions, has struck a climate change agreement with the United States, is working to combat piracy on the high seas, and is taking an active role in shaping Afghanistan's future. The two countries continue to negotiate a bilateral investment treaty, and China has even expressed interest in the TPP, but the agenda for economic cooperation, though a potential bright spot in the relationship, may stall if China grows even more skeptical of reforms in the wake of the recent economic retrenchment. On security matters, the United States and China should take steps to insulate military exchanges from political swings in the bilateral relationship and develop them into vehicles for discussing the region's security challenges.

Ninth, even as it looks for areas of cooperation, the United States should make clear that any attempt by China to challenge fundamental U.S. national interests in Asia will be met by resolute resistance and will not advance Chinese grand strategy. The United States should declare its determination to retain a seat at the table in those organizations that discuss Asia's future and oppose China's efforts to elevate or build important organizations that do not include the United States, such as CICA, the Shanghai Cooperation Organization, and—at least until the United States was invited to join in 2011—the East Asia Summit. The United States should also continue to explicitly challenge and vocally denounce Chinese policies that would limit freedom of navigation by insisting on long-standing international legal norms for both civilian and military traffic. To that end, the United States should continue to use military assets to challenge unilateral applications of Chinese sovereignty in disputed areas. With regard to Chinese cyber hacking, the United States should monitor the commitments Xi made during his visit to Washington to cease the theft of intellectual property for commercial gain and to refrain from attacks on critical infrastructure during peacetime. Some reports suggest that China has already failed to live up to its recent pledges. If it does not make an effort to honor its commitment in coming months, the United States should be prepared to respond with biting financial sanctions on those individuals and entities engaging in theft as well as those companies directly benefiting from it.[54]

Finally, the United States should revitalize the sources of its own national power.[55] Even if it falls short of substantially reducing internecine partisan conflict, the United States can at least attempt to avoid self-inflicted wounds such as the sequester of defense spending, opposition to the TPP, the near shuttering of the Export-Import Bank, and chronic underinvestment in infrastructure and human capital. The United States will also need to make progress on long overdue domestic policy priorities, including reforms of the immigration system and entitlement spending. With a sound long-term economy, skillful military and diplomatic initiatives, as well as a more productive domestic political environment, Washington can ensure that the United States remains the most powerful and influential nation in Asia. That grand strategic outcome would be the best recipe for ensuring that the current positive balance of power is sustained in the region, that Xi Jinping's more assertive foreign and defense policies are sufficiently shaped by the United States with its allies and friends to avoid a U.S.-China confrontation, and that Asia fulfills its extraordinary promise in the decades ahead.

Some of these suggested policies may seem familiar and most have been debated in public discourse in recent years. Thus prescriptive familiarity is not the problem with respect to U.S. policies toward Asia. Rather, it is that most such efforts have seen too little policy intensity and policy follow-through. Recent administrations have given insufficient attention to policy propositions regarding the United States and Asia and spent the majority of top-level time and effort confronting the never-ending crises of the Middle East—from Saddam Hussein through Iran to the so-called Islamic State.

Even when U.S. presidents do manage to find time for much-needed trips to Asia, these cannot substitute for high-level and consistent policy focus.[56] In the words of Lee Kuan Yew, "You Americans seem to think that dealing with Asia is like freezing a frame of a movie. While you turn your attention elsewhere, you imagine that nothing moves out here until you once again remember us. We cannot seem to persuade you that Asia is not like that, and that China is here every day."[57]

Meanwhile, China, not burdened by global security responsibilities, benefits strategically as the United States is pulled into one Middle Eastern morass after another at the expense of its Asian policy priorities. What is therefore required is not the occasional administration speech in a Washington think tank touting the importance of Asia, but instead that U.S. policymakers recognize every day that the primary engines of the world economy and the challenge to American primacy are not in the Middle East or Europe but have shifted to Asia. This energized American pivot to Asia is the indispensable ingredient in a successful U.S. policy to participate and project strength more consequentially in the region and to deal with Chinese power and influence under Xi Jinping.

Endnotes

1. For an extended analysis of China's use of the geoeconomic instrument, see Robert D. Blackwill and Jennifer M. Harris, *War by Other Means: Geoeconomics and Statecraft* (Cambridge, MA: Harvard University Press, April 2016).
2. See Kurt M. Campbell, *The Pivot*, forthcoming.
3. "Xi Says China Needs at Least 6.5% Growth in Next Five Years," Bloomberg, November 3, 2015, http://www.bloomberg.com/news/articles/2015-11-03/xi-says-china-needs-no-less-than-6-5-growth-in-next-five-years. See also Luke Kawa, "Six Ways to Gauge How Fast China's Economy Is Actually Growing," Bloomberg, November 2, 2015, http://www.bloomberg.com/news/articles/2015-11-02/six-ways-to-gauge-how-fast-china-s-economy-is-actually-growing. For another survey of professional forecasts, see Josh Noble, "Doubts Rise over China's Official GDP Growth Rate," *Financial Times*, September 16, 2015, http://www.ft.com/cms/s/0/723a8d8e-5c53-11e5-9846-de406ccb37f2.html#axzz3uVUQ0j3B.
4. Richard Baum, *Burying Mao* (Princeton, NJ: Princeton University Press, 1996).
5. Christopher K. Johnson and Scott Kennedy, "China's Un-Separation of Powers," *Foreign Affairs*, July 24, 2015, https://www.foreignaffairs.com/articles/china/2015-07-24/chinas-un-separation-powers.
6. Ibid.
7. These figures are Li Zhanshu and Cai Qi. See Keith Zhai and Zhang Hong, "Xi Jinping Ally Cai Qi to Have Senior Role at National Security Commission," *South China Morning Post*, March 28, 2014, http://www.scmp.com/news/china/article/1458826/xi-jinping-ally-cai-qi-have-senior-role-national-security-commission.
8. Chris Buckley, "China Arrests Ex-Chief of Domestic Security in Graft Case," *New York Times*, December 5, 2014, http://www.nytimes.com/2014/12/06/world/asia/zhou-yongkang-china-arrests-former-security-chief.html?_r=0.
9. Jeremy Page and Brian Spegele, "Chinese Communist Party Ousts a Former General," *Wall Street Journal*, June 30, 2014, http://www.wsj.com/articles/chinese-communist-party-ousts-a-former-top-general-on-bribe-taking-allegations-1404126279.
10. "Xi Stresses Military Headquarters' Loyalty to Party," *China Daily*, September 22, 2014, http://www.chinadaily.com.cn/china/2014-09/22/content_18641532.htm; Cary Huang, "Xi Jinping Orders PLA to Step Up Its 'Real Combat' Awareness," *South China Morning Post*, December 13, 2012, http://www.scmp.com/news/china/article/1103957/xi-jinping-orders-pla-step-its-real-combat-awareness.
11. "Xi Stresses CPC's Absolute Leadership Over Army," *China Daily*, November 3, 2014, http://www.chinadaily.com.cn/m/fujian/longyan/2014-11/03/content_18954259.htm.
12. Evan Osnos, "Born Red," *New Yorker*, April 6, 2015, http://www.newyorker.com/magazine/2015/04/06/born-red.

13. Andrew Jacobs and Chris Buckley, "Move Over Mao: Beloved 'Papa Xi' Awes China," *New York Times*, March 7, 2015, http://www.nytimes.com/2015/03/08/world/move-over-mao-beloved-papa-xi-awes-china.html.

14. Tony Saich, "Reflections on a Survey of Global Perceptions of International Leaders and World Powers," Harvard Kennedy School's Ash Center for Democratic Governance and Innovation, December 2014, http://ash.harvard.edu/files/ash/files/survey-global-perceptions-international-leaders-world-powers_0.pdf.

15. Osnos, "Born Red."

16. Jeremy Page, "China Spins New Lesson From Soviet Union's Fall," *Wall Street Journal*, December 10, 2013, http://www.wsj.com/articles/SB10001424052702303755504579207070196382560; Willy Wo-Lap Lam, *Chinese Politics in the Era of Xi Jinping: Renaissance, Reform, or Retrogression?* (London: Routledge, 2015), 75–150; see also the piece informed by Roderick MacFarquhar's views, Simon Denyer, "Twin Historic Traumas Shape Xi Jinping's China Presidency," *Washington Post*, March 2, 2015, https://www.washingtonpost.com/world/asia_pacific/twin-historical-traumas-shape-xi-jinpings-china-presidency/2015/03/02/b4074516-b2f0-11e4-bf39-5560f3918d4b_story.html.

17. Osnos, "Born Red."

18. Gabriel Wildau, "China Migration: At the Turning Point," *Financial Times*, May 4, 2015, http://www.ft.com/intl/cms/s/2/767495a0-e99b-11e4-b863-00144feab7de.html#axzz3kGXj4Ocg.

19. Bruce Einhorn, "In China, Shirtmaker TAL Uses Data Analysis for Efficiency Boost," *Bloomberg Businessweek*, January 8, 2015, http://www.bloomberg.com/news/articles/2015-01-08/chinas-shirt-factories-invest-in-efficiency-as-wages-rise; Chun Han Wong, "As China's Economy Slows, So Too Does Growth in Workers' Wages," *Wall Street Journal*, December 17, 2014, http://blogs.wsj.com/chinarealtime/2014/12/17/as-chinas-economy-slows-so-too-does-growth-in-workers-wages/; Mark Magnier, "China's Productivity Problem Drags on Growth," *Wall Street Journal*, September 1, 2014, http://blogs.wsj.com/economics/2014/09/01/chinas-productivity-problem-drags-on-growth/.

20. Brian Bremner, "Is China Coming Back Down to Earth?," *Bloomberg Business*, January 22, 2015, http://www.bloomberg.com/bw/articles/2015-01-22/china-s-risks-in-shedding-debt-fueled-investment-led-growth#p1.

21. Richard Dobbs, Susan Lund, Jonathan Woetzel, and Mina Mutafchieva, *Debt and (Not Much) Deleveraging* (New York: McKinsey Global Institute, February 2015), http://www.mckinsey.com/insights/economic_studies/debt_and_not_much_deleveraging.

22. See estimates from Capital Economics, "China Economics Update," September 16, 2015, https://www.capitaleconomics.com/china-economics/china-economics-update/soe-reform-plan-falls-short; see also Shen Hong, "China's Small Businesses Lose Out on Cheaper Loans," *Wall Street Journal*, April 1, 2015, http://www.wsj.com/articles/chinas-small-businesses-lose-out-on-cheaper-loans-1427860298.

23. For a good primer, see "Taking a Tumble," *Economist*, August 29, 2015, http://www.economist.com/news/briefing/21662581-stockmarket-turmoil-china-need-not-spell-economic-doom-it-does-raise-questions-far.

24. "Xi Jinping's Bull Market," *Wall Street Journal*, April 16, 2015, http://www.wsj.com/articles/xi-jinpings-bull-market-1429228912.

25. Keith Bradsher, "China Turned to Risky Devaluation as Export Machine Stalled," *New York Times*, August 17, 2015, http://www.nytimes.com/2015/08/18/business/international/chinas-devaluation-of-its-currency-was-a-call-to-action.html?_r=0; "China Detains Labor Activists as Number of Workplace Disputes Doubles,"

NBCnews.com, December 22, 2015, http://www.nbcnews.com/business/economy/china-detains-labor-activists-number-workplace-disputes-doubles-n484426.

26. Edward Wong, "Consumer Anxiety in China Undermines Government's Plans," *New York Times*, August 28, 2015, http://www.nytimes.com/2015/08/29/world/asia/consumer-anxiety-in-china-undermines-governments-economic-plans.html.

27. The term *mass incident* is used by the Chinese government to refer to protests and disputes involving large groups of people.

28. This has long been a deeply held Chinese belief, and Premier Wen Jiabao reaffirmed it in 2009. See "China Sets 8% Growth Target to Maintain Social Order," *Sydney Morning Herald*, January 29, 2009, http://www.smh.com.au/business/china-sets-8-growth-target-to-maintain-social-order-20090128-7s5x.html.

29. Lingling Wei, "China Unveils Economic Blueprint for 2016," *Wall Street Journal*, December 21, 2015, http://www.wsj.com/articles/china-set-to-unveil-economic-blueprint-for-2016-1450691139.

30. Michael Forsythe and Jonathan Ansfield, "Fading Economy and Graft Crackdown Rattle China's Leadership," *New York Times*, August 22, 2015, http://www.nytimes.com/2015/08/23/world/asia/chinas-economy-and-graft-crackdown-rattle-leaders.html; Jeremy Page and Lingling Wei, "Crises Put First Dents in Xi Jinping's Power," *Wall Street Journal*, August 30, 2015, http://www.wsj.com/articles/crises-put-first-dents-in-xi-jinpings-power-1440977618.

31. Peter Hays Gries, *China's New Nationalism: Pride, Politics, and Diplomacy* (Oakland: University of California Press, 2005).

32. "Xi Calls for Patriotism in Achieving Chinese Dream," Xinhua, December 30, 2015, news.xinhuanet.com/english/2015-12/30/c_134965704.htm.

33. Shi Yinhong, "China's Complicated Foreign Policy," European Council on Foreign Relations, March 31, 2015, http://www.ecfr.eu/article/commentary_chinas_complicated_foreign_policy311562.

34. Brian Spegele and Vu Trong Khanh, "Vietnam Spat Represents a Chinese Leap," *Wall Street Journal*, May 8, 2014, http://www.wsj.com/articles/SB10001424052702304655304579549330994442014.

35. "Malaysia to Protest Over Chinese Coast Guard 'Intruders': WSJ," Reuters, June 9, 2015, http://www.reuters.com/article/2015/06/09/us-southchinasea-malaysia-china-idUSKBN0OP06120150609; see also Prashanth Parameswaran, "Playing It Safe: Malaysia's Approach to the South China Sea and Implications for the United States," Center for a New American Security Maritime Strategy Series, February 2015, http://www.cnas.org/sites/default/files/publications-pdf/CNAS%20Maritime%206_Parameswaran_Final.pdf.

36. U.S. Department of Defense, "Asia-Pacific Maritime Security Strategy," Summer 2015, p. 16, http://www.defense.gov/Portals/1/Documents/pubs/NDAA%20A-P_Maritime_SecuritY_Strategy-08142015-1300-FINALFORMAT.PDF; Matthew Rosenberg, "China Deployed Artillery on Disputed Island, U.S. Says," *New York Times*, May 29, 2015, http://www.nytimes.com/2015/05/30/world/asia/chinese-artillery-spotted-on-spratly-island.html.

37. Kurt M. Campbell, "Trouble at Sea Reveals the New Shape of China's Foreign Policy," *Financial Times*, July 22, 2014, http://blogs.ft.com/the-a-list/2014/07/22/trouble-at-sea-reveals-the-new-shape-of-chinas-foreign-policy/.

38. Michael D. Swaine, "Chinese Views and Commentary on the 'One Belt, One Road' Initiative," *China Leadership Monitor* 47, http://www.hoover.org/sites/default/files/research/docs/clm47ms.pdf.

39. "China's Xi Jinping Signs Landmark Deals on India Visit," BBC, September 18, 2014, http://www.bbc.com/news/world-asia-india-29249268.

40. Jane Perlez, "Xi Jinping Heads to Pakistan, Bearing Billions in Infrastructure Aid," *New York Times*, April 19, 2015, http://www.nytimes.com/2015/04/20/world/asia/chinas-president-heads-to-pakistan-with-billions-in-infrastructure-aid.html; for a larger overview of China-India competition in the Indian Ocean region, see C. Raja Mohan, *Samudra Manthan: Sino-Indian Rivalry in the Indo-Pacific* (Washington, DC: Carnegie Endowment for International Peace, 2012).

41. Michael Forsythe, "China Refuses to Confirm Okinawa Island Belongs to Japanese," *Bloomberg Business*, May 8, 2013, http://www.bloomberg.com/news/articles/2013-05-08/china-scholars-say-okinawa-s-ownership-may-be-in-question-1-.

42. Jane Perlez, "Xi Jinping's U.S. Visit," *New York Times*, September 28, 2015, http://www.nytimes.com/interactive/projects/cp/reporters-notebook/xi-jinping-visit.

43. Alwyn Scott and Eric M. Johnson, "Boeing Wins $38 Billion in Orders, Commitments from China," Reuters, September 23, 2015, http://www.reuters.com/article/us-boeing-china-idUSKCN0RM27X20150923.

44. Joseph Menn, "China Tried to Hack U.S. Firms Even After Cyber Pact–Crowd Strike," Reuters, October 19, 2015, http://www.reuters.com/article/2015/10/19/usa-china-cybersecurity-idUSL1N12J01Q20151019.

45. Andrew Browne, "What Xi Jinping Offered in the U.S.: A Slight Shift in Tone," *Wall Street Journal*, September 29, 2015, http://www.wsj.com/articles/what-xi-jinping-offered-in-the-u-s-a-slight-shift-in-tone-1443503759.

46. Bonnie Glaser and Jacqueline Vitello, "Xi Jinping's Great Game: Are China and Taiwan Headed Towards Trouble?" *National Interest*, July 16, 2015, http://nationalinterest.org/feature/xi-jinpings-great-game-are-china-taiwan-headed-towards-13346.

47. Javier C. Hernandez, "After Nuclear Test, China Resists Pressure to Curb North Korea," *New York Times*, January 15, 2016, http://www.nytimes.com/2016/01/16/world/asia/north-korea-xi-jinping-obama.html.

48. Noted sinologist Susan Shirk has made this point cogently.

49. Robert D. Blackwill and Ashley J. Tellis, *Revising U.S. Grand Strategy Toward China*, Council Special Report no. 72 (New York: Council on Foreign Relations, April 2015).

50. Michael D. Shear, "With China in Mind on a Visit to Manila, Obama Pledges Military Aid to Allies in Southeast Asia," *New York Times*, November 17, 2015, http://www.nytimes.com/2015/11/18/world/asia/obama-philippines-south-china-sea-military-aidship.html.

51. Charles R. Kaye, Joseph S. Nye Jr., and Alyssa Ayres, *Working with a Rising India: A Joint Venture for the New Century*, Independent Task Force Report no. 73 (Washington, DC: Council on Foreign Relations, November 2015), p. 3.

52. The following were adapted from the proposals put forward in Blackwill and Tellis's *Revising U.S. Grand Strategy Toward China*.

53. Blackwill and Harris, *War by Other Means*.

54. See Blackwill and Tellis, *Revising U.S. Grand Strategy Toward China*.

55. Richard Haass, *Foreign Policy Begins at Home: The Case for Putting America's House in Order* (New York: Basic Books, 2013).

56. Gardiner Harris, "Foreign-Policy Trips Fill Obama's Schedule for Final Year," *New York Times*, January 2, 2016, http://www.nytimes.com/2016/01/03/us/foreign-policy-trips-fill-obamas-schedule-for-final-year.html.

57. Discussion with Robert Blackwill.

About the Authors

Robert Blackwill is Henry A. Kissinger senior fellow for U.S. foreign policy at the Council on Foreign Relations (CFR). His current work focuses on U.S. foreign policy writ large as well as on China, Russia, the Middle East, South Asia, and geoeconomics. Blackwill served as counselor to CFR in 2005. Most recently, he was senior fellow at the RAND Corporation in Santa Monica, California, from 2008 to 2010, after serving from 2004 to 2008 as president of BGR International. As deputy assistant to the president and deputy national security advisor for strategic planning under President George W. Bush, Blackwill was responsible for government-wide policy planning to help develop and coordinate the mid- and long-term direction of U.S. foreign policy. He also served as presidential envoy to Iraq and was the administration's coordinator for U.S. policies regarding Afghanistan and Iran. Blackwill went to the National Security Council (NSC) after serving as the U.S. ambassador to India from 2001 to 2003. He is the recipient of the 2007 Bridge-Builder Award for his role in transforming U.S.-India relations, and the 2016 Padma Bhushan award from the government of India for distinguished service of a high order.

Prior to reentering government in 2001, Blackwill was the Belfer lecturer in international security at Harvard Kennedy School. During his fourteen years as a Harvard faculty member, he was associate dean of the Kennedy School, where he taught foreign and defense policy and public policy analysis. He was faculty chair for executive training programs for business and government leaders from Saudi Arabia, Kuwait, the Palestinian Authority, Israel, and Kazakhstan, as well as military general officers from Russia and the People's Republic of China. From 1989 to 1990, he was special assistant to President George H.W. Bush for European and Soviet affairs, during which time he was awarded the Commander's Cross of the Order of Merit by the Federal Republic of Germany for his contribution to German unification. Earlier in his career, he was the U.S. ambassador to conventional arms negotiations with the Warsaw Pact, director for European affairs at the NSC, principal deputy assistant secretary of state for political-military affairs, and principal deputy assistant secretary of state for European affairs.

Blackwill is author and editor of many articles and books on transatlantic relations, Russia and the West, the Greater Middle East, and Asian security. He edited the CFR book *Iran: The Nuclear Challenge*. His best-selling book coauthored with Graham Allison of the Harvard Kennedy School, titled *Lee Kuan Yew: The Grand Master's Insights on China, the United States, and the World*, has sold 180,000 copies. He coauthored, with Ashley J. Tellis of the Carnegie Endowment, the Council Special Report *Revising U.S. Grand Strategy Toward China*. His newest book, *War by Other Means: Geoeconomics and Statecraft*, coauthored with Jennifer M. Harris, will be published in April 2016 by Belknap Press, an imprint of Harvard University Press. Blackwill is a member of the Council on Foreign Relations, the International Institute for Strategic Studies, and the Aspen Strategy Group; a nonresident senior fellow and on the international board of Harvard University's Belfer Center for Science and International Affairs; senior advisor to the rector of Kazakhstan's New Economic University; and on the board of the American University of Iraq, Suleimani.

Kurt M. Campbell is chairman and chief executive officer of the Asia Group, LLC. He also serves as chairman of the Center for a New American Security, is a nonresident fellow at Harvard Kennedy School's Belfer Center for Science and International Affairs, and is on the board of directors for Standard Chartered PLC in London. From 2009 to 2013, he served as the assistant secretary of state for East Asian and Pacific affairs, where he is widely credited as being an architect of the "pivot to Asia." For his work, Secretary Hillary Clinton awarded him the Secretary of State's Distinguished Service Award, the nation's highest diplomatic honor. Campbell served as an honorary officer of the Order of Australia and as an honorary companion of the New Zealand Order of Merit for his work in support of U.S. relations with Australia and New Zealand, respectively. He also received top national honors from Korea and Taiwan.

Campbell was formerly the chief executive officer and cofounder of the Center for a New American Security and concurrently served as the director of the Aspen Strategy Group and chairman of the editorial board of the *Washington Quarterly*. He was the founder and chairman of StratAsia and was previously the senior vice president, director of the International Security Program, and Henry A. Kissinger chair at the Center for Strategic and International Studies. Campbell was also associate professor of public policy and international relations at the Harvard Kennedy School and assistant director of Harvard University's Center for Science and International Affairs. He served as the vice chairman of the Pentagon Memorial Fund and sat on the board of directors of Metlife, Inc., of New York.

Campbell previously served as deputy assistant secretary of defense for Asia and the Pacific, director on the National Security Council staff, deputy special counselor to the president for North American Free Trade Agreement in the White House, and White House fellow at the Department of the Treasury. Formerly an officer in the U.S. Navy reserves, he has received Georgetown University's Asia Service Award, the State Department Honor Award, the Republic of Korea medal for service, and the Department of Defense Medals for Distinguished Public Service and for Outstanding Public Service.

He is the author or editor of ten books, including *Difficult Transitions: Why Presidents Fail in Foreign Policy at the Outset of Power* (2008) and *Hard Power: The New Politics of National Security* (2006). He is currently writing a book about his experiences and U.S.-Asia policy titled *The Pivot: The Future of American Statecraft in Asia*.

Campbell received his bachelor's degree from the University of California, San Diego, a certificate in music and political philosophy from the University of Erevan in Soviet Armenia, and his doctorate in international relations from Brasenose College at Oxford University, where he was a Distinguished Marshall Scholar.

Members of 2014–2015 Study Group on Chinese Foreign Policy

Graham T. Allison
Harvard Kennedy School's Belfer Center for Science & International Affairs

Brian Andrews
Asia Group, LLC

Alyssa Ayres, *ex officio*
Council on Foreign Relations

Samuel R. Berger
Albright Stonebridge Group

Stephen E. Biegun
Ford Motor Company

Benjamin T. Brake
U.S. Department of State

Cameron Ray Chen
Joint Chiefs of Staff

Eliot A. Cohen
Johns Hopkins School of Advanced International Studies

Richard Danzig
Center for a New American Security

Jacqueline Newmyer Deal
Long Term Strategy Group

Patrick Dewar
Lockheed Martin Corporation

Douglas J. Feith
Hudson Institute

Ellen L. Frost
East-West Center

Bonnie S. Glaser
Center for Strategic and International Studies

Michael J. Green
Center for Strategic and International Studies

Stephen J. Hadley
RiceHadleyGates, LLC

Ziad Haider
U.S. Department of State

Susan J. Jakes
Asia Society

Richard C. Jao
U.S. Department of State

Christopher K. Johnson
Center for Strategic and International Studies

David M. Lampton
Johns Hopkins University's School of Advanced International Studies

Kenneth G. Lieberthal
Brookings Institution

Leo Sidney Mackay
Lockheed Martin Corporation

James H. Mann
Johns Hopkins University's School of Advanced International Studies

Daniel S. Markey, *ex officio*
Council on Foreign Relations

David H. McCormick
Bridgewater Associates, LP

Michael A. McDevitt
Center for Naval Analyses

Richard McGregor
Wilson Center for Public Research

Evan S. Medeiros
Eurasia Group

Michael O'Hanlon
Brookings Institution

J. J. Ong
Chevron Corporation

Evan L. R. Osnos
New Yorker

Jonathan D. Pollack
Brookings Institution

Mira Rapp-Hooper
Center for a New American Security

Ely Ratner
Office of the Vice President

J. Stapleton Roy
*Woodrow Wilson International Center
for Scholars*

David Shambaugh
*George Washington University's Elliot School
of International Affairs*

Andrew Small
German Marshall Fund of the United States

Richard H. Solomon
RAND Corporation

Robert S. Spalding
Joint Chiefs of Staff

Jennifer Bulkeley Staats
Office of the Secretary of Defense

Paul B. Stares, *ex officio*
Council on Foreign Relations

Jonathan R. Stromseth
U.S. Department of State

Robert G. Sutter
*George Washington University's Elliot School
of International Affairs*

Allan Wendt
Strategic Technology Policy

Thomas Straus Wyler
U.S. Department of Commerce

Ali Wyne
RAND Corporation

Andrew I. Yeo
Catholic University of America

We are in debt to the members of the CFR study group on Chinese foreign policy for their comments and critiques on our draft report, all of which improved the substance of the final text. This report reflects the judgments and recommendations of the authors. It does not necessarily represent the views of members of the study group, whose involvement in no way should be interpreted as an endorsement of the report by either themselves or the organizations with which they are affiliated.

Mission Statement of the International Institutions and Global Governance Program

The International Institutions and Global Governance (IIGG) program at CFR aims to identify the institutional requirements for effective multilateral cooperation in the twenty-first century. The program is motivated by recognition that the architecture of global governance—largely reflecting the world as it existed in 1945—has not kept pace with fundamental changes in the international system. These shifts include the spread of transnational challenges, the rise of new powers, and the mounting influence of nonstate actors. Existing multilateral arrangements thus provide an inadequate foundation for addressing many of today's most pressing threats and opportunities and for advancing U.S. national and broader global interests.

Given these trends, U.S. policymakers and other interested actors require rigorous, independent analysis of current structures of multilateral cooperation, and of the promises and pitfalls of alternative institutional arrangements. The IIGG program meets these needs by analyzing the strengths and weaknesses of existing multilateral institutions and proposing reforms tailored to new international circumstances.

The IIGG program fulfills its mandate by

- Engaging CFR fellows in research on improving existing and building new frameworks to address specific global challenges—including climate change, the proliferation of weapons of mass destruction, transnational terrorism, and global health—and disseminating the research through books, articles, Council Special Reports, and other outlets;

- Bringing together influential foreign policymakers, scholars, and CFR members to debate the merits of international regimes and frameworks at meetings in New York, Washington, DC, and other select cities;

- Hosting roundtable series whose objectives are to inform the foreign policy community of today's international governance challenges and breed inventive solutions to strengthen the world's multilateral bodies; and

- Providing a state-of-the-art Web presence as a resource to the wider foreign policy community on issues related to the future of global governance.

Council Special Reports

Published by the Council on Foreign Relations

Partners in Preventive Action: The United States and International Institutions
Paul B. Stares and Micah Zenko; CSR No. 62, September 2011
A Center for Preventive Action Report

Justice Beyond The Hague: Supporting the Prosecution of International Crimes in National Courts
David A. Kaye; CSR No. 61, June 2011

The Drug War in Mexico: Confronting a Shared Threat
David A. Shirk; CSR No. 60, March 2011
A Center for Preventive Action Report

UN Security Council Enlargement and U.S. Interests
Kara C. McDonald and Stewart M. Patrick; CSR No. 59, December 2010
An International Institutions and Global Governance Program Report

Congress and National Security
Kay King; CSR No. 58, November 2010

Toward Deeper Reductions in U.S. and Russian Nuclear Weapons
Micah Zenko; CSR No. 57, November 2010
A Center for Preventive Action Report

Internet Governance in an Age of Cyber Insecurity
Robert K. Knake; CSR No. 56, September 2010
An International Institutions and Global Governance Program Report

From Rome to Kampala: The U.S. Approach to the 2010 International Criminal Court Review Conference
Vijay Padmanabhan; CSR No. 55, April 2010

Strengthening the Nuclear Nonproliferation Regime
Paul Lettow; CSR No. 54, April 2010
An International Institutions and Global Governance Program Report

The Russian Economic Crisis
Jeffrey Mankoff; CSR No. 53, April 2010

Somalia: A New Approach
Bronwyn E. Bruton; CSR No. 52, March 2010
A Center for Preventive Action Report

The Future of NATO
James M. Goldgeier; CSR No. 51, February 2010
An International Institutions and Global Governance Program Report

The United States in the New Asia
Evan A. Feigenbaum and Robert A. Manning; CSR No. 50, November 2009
An International Institutions and Global Governance Program Report

Intervention to Stop Genocide and Mass Atrocities: International Norms and U.S. Policy
Matthew C. Waxman; CSR No. 49, October 2009
An International Institutions and Global Governance Program Report

Enhancing U.S. Preventive Action
Paul B. Stares and Micah Zenko; CSR No. 48, October 2009
A Center for Preventive Action Report

The Canadian Oil Sands: Energy Security vs. Climate Change
Michael A. Levi; CSR No. 47, May 2009
A Maurice R. Greenberg Center for Geoeconomic Studies Report

The National Interest and the Law of the Sea
Scott G. Borgerson; CSR No. 46, May 2009

Lessons of the Financial Crisis
Benn Steil; CSR No. 45, March 2009
A Maurice R. Greenberg Center for Geoeconomic Studies Report

Global Imbalances and the Financial Crisis
Steven Dunaway; CSR No. 44, March 2009
A Maurice R. Greenberg Center for Geoeconomic Studies Report

Eurasian Energy Security
Jeffrey Mankoff; CSR No. 43, February 2009

Preparing for Sudden Change in North Korea
Paul B. Stares and Joel S. Wit; CSR No. 42, January 2009
A Center for Preventive Action Report

Averting Crisis in Ukraine
Steven Pifer; CSR No. 41, January 2009
A Center for Preventive Action Report

Congo: Securing Peace, Sustaining Progress
Anthony W. Gambino; CSR No. 40, October 2008
A Center for Preventive Action Report

Deterring State Sponsorship of Nuclear Terrorism
Michael A. Levi; CSR No. 39, September 2008

China, Space Weapons, and U.S. Security
Bruce W. MacDonald; CSR No. 38, September 2008

Sovereign Wealth and Sovereign Power: The Strategic Consequences of American Indebtedness
Brad W. Setser; CSR No. 37, September 2008
A Maurice R. Greenberg Center for Geoeconomic Studies Report

Securing Pakistan's Tribal Belt
Daniel S. Markey; CSR No. 36, July 2008 (web-only release) and August 2008
A Center for Preventive Action Report

Avoiding Transfers to Torture
Ashley S. Deeks; CSR No. 35, June 2008

Global FDI Policy: Correcting a Protectionist Drift
David M. Marchick and Matthew J. Slaughter; CSR No. 34, June 2008
A Maurice R. Greenberg Center for Geoeconomic Studies Report

Dealing with Damascus: Seeking a Greater Return on U.S.-Syria Relations
Mona Yacoubian and Scott Lasensky; CSR No. 33, June 2008
A Center for Preventive Action Report

Climate Change and National Security: An Agenda for Action
Joshua W. Busby; CSR No. 32, November 2007
A Maurice R. Greenberg Center for Geoeconomic Studies Report

Planning for Post-Mugabe Zimbabwe
Michelle D. Gavin; CSR No. 31, October 2007
A Center for Preventive Action Report

The Case for Wage Insurance
Robert J. LaLonde; CSR No. 30, September 2007
A Maurice R. Greenberg Center for Geoeconomic Studies Report

Reform of the International Monetary Fund
Peter B. Kenen; CSR No. 29, May 2007
A Maurice R. Greenberg Center for Geoeconomic Studies Report

Nuclear Energy: Balancing Benefits and Risks
Charles D. Ferguson; CSR No. 28, April 2007

Nigeria: Elections and Continuing Challenges
Robert I. Rotberg; CSR No. 27, April 2007
A Center for Preventive Action Report

The Economic Logic of Illegal Immigration
Gordon H. Hanson; CSR No. 26, April 2007
A Maurice R. Greenberg Center for Geoeconomic Studies Report

The United States and the WTO Dispute Settlement System
Robert Z. Lawrence; CSR No. 25, March 2007
A Maurice R. Greenberg Center for Geoeconomic Studies Report

Bolivia on the Brink
Eduardo A. Gamarra; CSR No. 24, February 2007
A Center for Preventive Action Report

After the Surge: The Case for U.S. Military Disengagement From Iraq
Steven N. Simon; CSR No. 23, February 2007

Darfur and Beyond: What Is Needed to Prevent Mass Atrocities
Lee Feinstein; CSR No. 22, January 2007

Avoiding Conflict in the Horn of Africa: U.S. Policy Toward Ethiopia and Eritrea
Terrence Lyons; CSR No. 21, December 2006
A Center for Preventive Action Report

Living with Hugo: U.S. Policy Toward Hugo Chávez's Venezuela
Richard Lapper; CSR No. 20, November 2006
A Center for Preventive Action Report

Reforming U.S. Patent Policy: Getting the Incentives Right
Keith E. Maskus; CSR No. 19, November 2006
A Maurice R. Greenberg Center for Geoeconomic Studies Report

Foreign Investment and National Security: Getting the Balance Right
Alan P. Larson and David M. Marchick; CSR No. 18, July 2006
A Maurice R. Greenberg Center for Geoeconomic Studies Report

Challenges for a Postelection Mexico: Issues for U.S. Policy
Pamela K. Starr; CSR No. 17, June 2006 (web-only release) and November 2006

U.S.-India Nuclear Cooperation: A Strategy for Moving Forward
Michael A. Levi and Charles D. Ferguson; CSR No. 16, June 2006

Generating Momentum for a New Era in U.S.-Turkey Relations
Steven A. Cook and Elizabeth Sherwood-Randall; CSR No. 15, June 2006

Peace in Papua: Widening a Window of Opportunity
Blair A. King; CSR No. 14, March 2006
A Center for Preventive Action Report

Neglected Defense: Mobilizing the Private Sector to Support Homeland Security
Stephen E. Flynn and Daniel B. Prieto; CSR No. 13, March 2006

Afghanistan's Uncertain Transition From Turmoil to Normalcy
Barnett R. Rubin; CSR No. 12, March 2006
A Center for Preventive Action Report

Preventing Catastrophic Nuclear Terrorism
Charles D. Ferguson; CSR No. 11, March 2006

Getting Serious About the Twin Deficits
Menzie D. Chinn; CSR No. 10, September 2005
A Maurice R. Greenberg Center for Geoeconomic Studies Report

Both Sides of the Aisle: A Call for Bipartisan Foreign Policy
Nancy E. Roman; CSR No. 9, September 2005

Forgotten Intervention? What the United States Needs to Do in the Western Balkans
Amelia Branczik and William L. Nash; CSR No. 8, June 2005
A Center for Preventive Action Report

A New Beginning: Strategies for a More Fruitful Dialogue with the Muslim World
Craig Charney and Nicole Yakatan; CSR No. 7, May 2005

Power-Sharing in Iraq
David L. Phillips; CSR No. 6, April 2005
A Center for Preventive Action Report

Giving Meaning to "Never Again": Seeking an Effective Response to the Crisis in Darfur and Beyond
Cheryl O. Igiri and Princeton N. Lyman; CSR No. 5, September 2004

Freedom, Prosperity, and Security: The G8 Partnership with Africa: Sea Island 2004 and Beyond
J. Brian Atwood, Robert S. Browne, and Princeton N. Lyman; CSR No. 4, May 2004

Addressing the HIV/AIDS Pandemic: A U.S. Global AIDS Strategy for the Long Term
Daniel M. Fox and Princeton N. Lyman; CSR No. 3, May 2004
Cosponsored with the Milbank Memorial Fund

Challenges for a Post-Election Philippines
Catharin E. Dalpino; CSR No. 2, May 2004
A Center for Preventive Action Report

Stability, Security, and Sovereignty in the Republic of Georgia
David L. Phillips; CSR No. 1, January 2004
A Center for Preventive Action Report

Note: Council Special Reports are available for download from CFR's website, www.cfr.org. For more information, email publications@cfr.org.

www.ingramcontent.com/pod-product-compliance
Lightning Source LLC
Chambersburg PA
CBHW060521280326
41933CB00014B/3056